I0192726

INHERITOR

Jeanine Stevens

FUTURECYCLE PRESS

www.futurecycle.org

Library of Congress Control Number: 2016939541

Copyright © 2016 Jeanine Stevens
All Rights Reserved

Published by FutureCycle Press
Lexington, Kentucky, USA

ISBN 978-1-942371-02-1

To Gregory
who helps me live in all the rooms.

Contents

Part I PETITION

Wintering Mushrooms..11
A Soft Garden.. 12
New Delhi.. 13
Mary's House—Ephesus... 14
In Tarsus..15
Petition.. 16
Swimming in the Aegean.. 17
Brunch Ghazal... 18
A Dish of Figs in Thrace... 19
Academic Options Ghazal... 20
Arabesque.. 21

Part II INVITATION

Where the River Fans Out..25
In Istanbul... 26
An Invitation..27
Pergamum Altar, Mysia.. 28
Preference.. 29
Caravanserais... 30
Barefoot.. 32
Writing a Ghazal in the Coffee Garden...................................... 33
Morning Coffee Ghazal... 34
What a Poem Can Do..35
Hodja's Story... 36
Prayer Rug Ghazal.. 37
Weather Change.. 38
Ecstasy Before Noon...39
Ghazal for Bar Soap..40

Part III FRAGMENTS

Aubade for Dark... 43
Inventions.. 44
Returning... 45
Salt Lick..46

American Bittern...47

House of Candlelight.. 48

Waste Ground... 50

Fragments... 51

Mythology... 52

Helen at the Scaean Gate... 53

Metropolitan... 54

Frond Ghazal.. 55

Part IV FOOT STONES

Breast Reliefs..59

Abundance of Light... 60

Kelp... 61

Calico...62

The Sound of Snow..63

Adornments.. 64

At the Ruins... 66

Manikin..67

Cave of Forgotten Dreams... 68

Vibrations...69

In the Sierras with Rumi.. 70

A Moment of Joy... 72

Five Nudes..73

Stars of the Summer Triangle..74

Minotaur Surprised while Eating....................................... 75

Retrieval.. 76

The Sultan's Ballroom.. 78

Angels in Summer.. 79

Moth and Lace.. 80

Genome Project... 82

Ordovician... 83

Slow Snapshots from a Fast- Moving Train..........................84

After a Few Years...86

Prufrock at the Coast..87

Notes

Acknowledgments

We must find our touchstones where we can.

—John Berryman

Part I
PETITION

Wintering Mushrooms

They gather over moist earth, clump
stout feet in dark mealy shade.

Are we like this too, waiting in deep
woods for a time release

surprised by our own abrupt appearance
in remote and unusual places?

And the winter squash, thick
and blue-white in autumn arrangements.

It seems the moon has nurtured this flesh
to reflect a glazed eye, a beauty rotund.

Sufficient unto themselves:
does it matter if they are eaten?

A Soft Garden

I survive on interiority,
the chipped enamel roasting pan,
library table, soft woods,
soft light, worn coverlet, papered walls,
skylights, locks, invisible bugs,
trap doors, momentary darkness—
my own dust.

I place five green apples, ignored
by visible insects, in a glass baking dish.
They hold such sweetness,
deserve to be graced with cinnamon,
butter and made crisp.

It seems such a basic right
to simply exist on one's home ground.
What of the Syrian woman
attacked in her home, no weapons on hand?
Inside the shelled dwelling,
     no news at all, only night
          and a *soft garden* scorched.

New Delhi

She is the brick wall that defines her,
the thin arms under the sari.
She is the madras pattern
of marigold orange and olive green.
She is the littered ground,
the ground scattered with bricks and refuse.
One brick is her table. She entertains
simply. There are no spoons,
only hands to mix grains and river water.
The street is her open window,
her furniture the battered chair tipped
on its side, a cupboard of sorts for bent pans.
She is the smoke-stained wall
and crouches under a large sign
in English, "Choice Shampoo."
She is the big toe that grips the ground.
Nearby are bits of denim,
foreign labels, and one bright, upright yellow pear.
Back straight, she does not slouch,
looks directly at the camera in a half smile.
She is the pierced diamond
carried in the side of her nose
and the red spice she holds to mix
with her evening meal. She is
the memory of golden flocks on hilly flanks,
the darkness of things being burnt
surrounded by things already burnt.
Her only book, a book of matches,
her tablet: the wall, her pen: bits of charcoal.
She doesn't worry if her seeds
are not planted by the spring equinox.

  —Photo, *National Geographic*

Mary's House—Ephesus

I think about my own devotion
and spotty church attendance
as we climb the hill to seclusion,
a safe haven where the apostle John
took Mary to live a life removed from danger.

In the small chapel, a few Muslims
have arrived before us and lie prostrate
before Mary's shrine.
They honor the mother of Jesus
as they honor mothers of all prophets.

I press through crowds to holy water,
unsure of the taste, yet just like the sulfur
in my deep well at home.

Looking back, I felt the memory
of hospitality, a dwelling within.

I'm relieved
I did not find her bed of stone.

In Tarsus

Strong colors, a backdrop of cream and orange buildings
in the sun. Tourists come to see a rubbled Roman road.
In my digital camera, a woman crouches behind a chain
link fence, watching. Almost hidden in large shrubs
heavy with summer's dust, she looks intently, peacock-
bright scarf, long-sleeved black dress. The childlike face
seems smooth but brows cut a deep crease between
gray eyes, lids tired as tulips' fallen petals. Hands grasp
the fence, hands asking for nothing. Rutted palms almost
obscure her lifelines. Nails short and scraggly, thumbs
enveloped in soft wrinkles, she could be an echo of ancient
tribes, inheritor of the bargain table. Perhaps a meek
survivor living here for centuries gathering impressions
of her own. I do not know who will inherit this earth
or who remembers the original trade routes. I do notice
the machine stitching on her cuff is expertly done.

Petition

For Lent, a healing tree stood in the sanctuary.
We wrote a name or condition
needing attention on a colored ribbon—green,
pink, lavender—then placed the silky strands in high branches.

I remember cathedrals in Mexico where peasant women
sold rosaries and replicas. Some candles were bent,
but I found a few new and unlit.

In Ohio, at the small Methodist Church built
with bricks donated by my great-great-grandfather,
I sat in quiet contemplation thinking
of other petitions:

    a note hastily written
           and cast off in a small stream,
      or folded in the chink of a wall,
         or tucked in rocks at Monterrey Bay,
            or torn and tossed into the air, carried off
            by gulls mistaking the bits for wafers.

It took a long time to compose the message
I secured in the netting at Mary's House in Ephesus.
"Peace in the family," a good place to start.
These were not big wars, just minor skirmishes,
but enough disruptions to make
you wonder about love and devotion.
What if I hadn't pressed for these things?

I will never know what works.
In the Mosque I remove my shoes, tuck curls
under a scarf blooming with crimson tulips.
I'm overcome by the brilliant cerulean blue tiles.

Swimming in the Aegean

Late afternoon, a small cove
against the cliff face. A ladder leads down to water
that holds antiquity. The far sea,

midnight blue, appears thick and heavy
yet close up, little surf, glassy.

Such joy on this glorious autumn
afternoon awash in Maxfield Parrish shades:
ornate urns, magic lamps, sunsets.

A healing sea pulls me
toward Atlantis—at the same time draws me back.

How can I leave after three days
where centuries thrived and languished?

A slight breeze. I hope to glimpse
Phoenicians, sails stained violet from crushed shells.

Yet today, no ships appear on my horizon.
only rosy dust from half-buried statues.

It's hard to believe
such luxury holds a corrosive, yet this Aegean
is also my curative, my one atonement.

Black shrouds blue; rough edges
nip velvety folds. Everyone has gone to dinner.

I only want crispy sardines
and heavily seasoned eggplant with mushrooms.

Brunch Ghazal

Naked disciples drag nets on the Sea of Tiberius.
Jesus sets up a BBQ. They all toast fish and bread.

In the southern hemisphere it is always tricky
to exchange ivory for diamonds, salt for gold.

I still have my Underwood Portable from high school.
A younger man calls me a seasoned poet. Spicy?

At camp I ate the undesirables, gorged on eggs
turned green in tin pans and slimy, fish-eyed tapioca.

At Pacific Bell, my first job, the supervisor, Miss Flowers,
had the hots for me. I disconnected Mickey Rooney thrice.

A brief walk at coffee break, we discover a hog wrapped
in burlap under the wooden bridge. Don't mention this.

A Dish of Figs in Thrace

I'm fascinated by the smooth skin,
the firm bulb-shape, green and velvety,
not withered or wrinkled like
the purple fruit from my childhood.

Hard to resist the very act of placement,
stacked in a pyramid, next to a bowl
of whitest yogurt and jellied pomegranate delights
studded with pistachios.

Teeth in, first bite, the structure
collapses into thick pith, seeded flesh exploding.
Scentless on the outside, inside, old earth's
faint perfume, and the color, a deeper mauve
seen only on painted jars from the east.

I eat too many, live four days on rice and water.
Figs preserve well, unlike the peach
and summer peace, so transient and brief.

It's late autumn. I'm not bothered
by the yellowing trees, scarlet leaves,
lolling heads of pumpkins in forgotten fields.

Resilient to bruising, symbol of longevity,
figs are meant for travel. I carry
a dozen in my pack. I vow to eat more.

Academic Options Ghazal

The melons are small but deep coral and sweet, the bread
unleavened, and tea strong as earth is served in small cups.

At lunch in Ankara, I watch new students enter the university
gates loaded with computers, posters, trunks and optimism.

Somewhere along the Silk Road, a woman is singing.
She bends down, delights to a find a discarded cell phone.

In a small bookshop in the Sierras, the owner drinks
a second pot of coffee and writes about his love for Siberia.

Noon on a Friday. Refuse trucks retreat, and gardeners
take away the noisy mowers. A crimson ash leaf hits the ground.

Inside Anatolia's hidden caves, stunning frescos gleam.
The call to prayer is unheard. Caravans don't travel this far.

Arabesque

In the first Autumn rain, I watch the aging Hawthorne,
berries crimson, so different from spring's chenille fluff.
The glisten and shine reminds me of Moorish
arabesque designs, intertwined geometrics, lush foliage.
I strived to master ballet's arabesque,
back arched, leg extended, stubborn musculature.
I try to emulate the stately white crane
in her winter thicket, neck strained to the sun.
How patterns repeat, reappear.
I think of Ingres' *Grande Odalisque*,
peach nude in striped turban reclining on her divan,
phoenix fan so casual in her hand. So different
from the odalisques in Alloula's *Colonial Harem*,
a collection of black-and-white postcards.
An Algerian woman poses on a mat,
empty tea cups wait, tumbled urn on its side.
And another from Kabyle, robe with slits where breasts
may be viewed. Her haughty glare haunts me.
I try to imagine the seedy garret she returns to each morning.
The Hawthorne still struggles through its cycles.
A large hole gapes in the narrow trunk;
gnarled branches twist from so many prunings.
Leaves will become bright russet, arms at the mercy
of January. Beauty repeated in disparate places,
beauty considered in the moment.

Part II
INVITATION

Where the River Fans Out

You may find a white feather
or remnants of salmon fighting to a place of origin.
Aggregates of stones in different structures
cause the water to change tones and octaves.
You want to keep walking, testing
each bend and inlet for other fugues, even a whisper
or sonnet; and when you tire,
here is a bench just for you.

You rest quietly; male deer step out of young oaks.
You wonder if the cluster of bluebirds
in the meadow was a mirage or a daydream.
Each flit of wing becomes a wish
for healing. Three young women you know
sit by the phone, wait for results.
Perhaps a white light
from the arced day moon will illuminate
their faces just for this brief moment.

As the brown rabbit cloaked in new fur rises
on hind feet, you think abundance.
From a distance, beaded eyes look at you, then past.
Leaving, you follow dusty tracks,
retrace the path that held all that blue,
that flurry of orange breast.
No sign, only tangled vines of wild grape.
When you return home, a lone
bluebird sings a minuet in your winter pear.

In Istanbul

A clear autumn morning, the police station explodes in Istanbul.
Sea bass flood fishing boats, then appear at the market
    in Istanbul.

At the ruins, hundreds of feral cats sip water from blue tiles.
The wooden horse is splintered and needs a polish near Istanbul.

My dress is Liz Claiborne from J. C. Penney's. Gypsy music,
the flute made of PVC pipe, and the wine flows free in Istanbul.

Atatürk's photo is cut from schoolbooks. When will the next
caravan arrive? Will the oil in our lanterns last the winter
    in Istanbul?

Droves of pumpkin vines encroach, encircle the old walls
    of Istanbul.
The Black Sea takes watch and orange heads loll at the gates
    in Istanbul.

An Invitation

What was the thought that woke me
in my wandering night mind,
an old lover appearing aged and wanting?

You drank Raki over calamari
and melon. I switched to wine.
We danced to gypsy music
accompanied by a modern clarinet.

Don't you remember the young goddess
in T-shirt and jeans moving toward
you, palms pressed tight?
There by the Bosporus, so humid
you wore a headband.

Almost sunrise, purple shadows
lace the lawn, grace cold statues.
The inkblot image wants to remain,
pulses on and off above Aphrodite Taverna.

I sip morning coffee.
Sense impressions fade as late-turning
constellations diminish in the light of a new star.

I remember the offer, an invitation
to travel on your caravan for six months.

       I had to say, "No."

Pergamum Altar, Mysia

The damage occurred
mid-century, remains moved to Berlin,
but Mysia is the place, the old site.
The young giant appears tormented, locked
ringlets, deep-cut marble eyes,
vacant sockets sunk to serpent legs.

Unclothed, dismantled, dying in disbelief,
he looks up at the goddess,
her sturdy body, flaxen gown in folds.
He longs to caress her knees, the ornate scrolled boots
laced for battle, the feathered laurel leaves
pressing sighs over her breasts.
She will not
          look at him.

      I think she loved the giant,
for one night exchanged hearts, danced on the altar—
she wearing his snakeskin mask, he, her shield.
I feel heat zones concentrate under ribs
and thighs, red flames smearing sunburn at midnight,

boots stomping out a last passion
scorching sand-gold dust. I want to be there,
transpose seared shapes into my own—
half an arm here, leg portion there—bring
tiger lilies and dancing shoes to remember the first days

     of my own thoughts.

Preference

You could be more than knees, elbows and freckles,
a voice lower than a frog. Spatula with chipped paint.

I will always prefer the oblong over the square, threshold
over the cornice to keep the diphthongs from the door.

And yes, the dunes over the trenches, the masked drama
over the comedy, the Chinese bluebonnets over the cactus,

the pantry over the formal dining room, the real ocean
off Key West over the big water tank at Universal Studios.

The prop girl repairs the leaky air tube on John Wayne's
dive suit. The black octopus is gone forever.

Caravanserais

A vast structure, once used to house camels on overnight
journeys across Anatolia.

Bright and humid, but cool
inside the courtyard.
I lie on a wide bench, sip water,
weak from too many green figs at breakfast.

Inside, drums begin, then flutes
and a stringed instrument: the *oud*,
with mother-of-pearl fretboard.

I take my seat in the front row with others,
pilgrims like me, respectful
and wide-eyed. I love us
all for our transitory innocence and need.

In still air
I begin to perspire
through my cotton shirt,
face dripping salt.

Rhythms continue as dervishes circle
the universe: a slow walk,
a measured pace,
then hems twirl, dip
and roll in celestial billows,
rise and fall in kaleidoscopes of stars.

I expect vertigo, but steadiness comes
with upturned palms.

Garments stir a dark breeze
that dries my forehead.

I return to the courtyard for strong tea
served in glass cups.
A gift shop with books and souvenirs
seems out of place,
but this is a land of bartering and bazaars.

Barefoot

Where your footsteps rest, there I want to be. —Rumi

The barge is coming,
bringing brazen foreigners
that should be banned
at the border, but local bistros
need the spirits they carry.
How bold, you might think,
but we have bided
our time and expect
those with broad backs
and burly chests
to sing in a foreign key.
We are women in a country
with too few men
and those who have one
won't share. The one
I want disembarks, barefoot,
a brass bell on his ankle.
The tinkling wakes
the early bats, a breath
of caves in blue air.
The sky grows dark,
blots out the sun.
The river burns gold.
I shake my ringlets,
show him where
my camel is tethered.

Writing a Ghazal in the Coffee Garden

I never liked the word *cohabit*. It seemed as if
one just dropped down into a room with a stranger.

Coalesce might be better, something in common,
like seafood, body language or the urge to flirt.

Your pajamas with the cowboy scenes, cactus
and ropes have to go. July is no time for flannel.

The roof opens to a leak. What sort of tool
kit did you bring, adze with a deep channel?

A lawyer draws up a cohabitation contract,
twelve pages and more costly than a will.

I don't fix more than two kinds of potatoes on Thanksgiving.
For domestic duties rendered, no compensation will be given.

I come home to find a favorite shrub chopped
to the ground. "I need closure," you say. You have it!

Someone painted the shutters a French blue. For a much
better view, I dust the silhouettes where photos used to sit.

      —for Rebecca

Morning Coffee Ghazal

I'm hooked on Juan Valdez for my morning shot of coffee.
Native Californians grind a local seed that resembles
    a bolder coffee.

We meet at Rick and Larry's, write, talk, eat and paint.
To the side, a gold and turquoise mural with sheiks
    enjoying our stronger coffee.

Joy shows the technique to construct a three-dimensional
snowflake out of copy paper. I cut, staple, create for two hours
    over morning coffee.

The nut oil mill in Provence chokes and smolders with fumes.
The olive oil mill in Tuscany offers hand cream
    and Galliano-laced coffee.

The anemic girl from Kentucky ate coffee by the spoonful.
Remember Nescafé? Shiny crystals still in use
    for strong instant coffee.

Sleeplessness digs into desired longevity. You bring
my robe, my Olympic Village mug.
    Ah! Steaming morning coffee.

What a Poem Can Do

A minute splinter lodges in my heel's tough part.
Needles and tweezers don't work.
Limping around, upsetting
balance, I'm certain it will infect and fester;
my spine will go
from walking akimbo,
my heart, from lack of exercise.

As a girl, anemic and prone to blood poisoning,
I remember long foot-soaks, my Dad finally
lancing the wound, my aunts hovering
at the doorway
(sepsis killed a younger brother).

Now in my tub, I sit
with both feet in hottest water,
brandy on ice in one hand,
Ovid's *The Amores* in the other,
then slather on Neosporin, apply a Band-Aid.

Hobbling around the kitchen, I fix
pulled pork in the crockpot, make coffee,
go back to bed, turn to a poem about trajectory,
reach down and flick
out pain with my thumbnail.

Hodja's Story

> I am on this caravan, like a tipsy camel
> I foam and froth. —Divani Shamsi Tabrizi

Hodja talks about camels spitting,
foaming, bright froth
dribbling
not in anger
but a response
to females in heat.
How simple the signal
for male arousal: no guessing, no
wasted time, no madness, no

                         hydrophobia.

(Hodja, a storyteller from Turkey)

Prayer Rug Ghazal

Harmonious, pitiless, boring dawn rouses us
to splintered treetops. Sticky sap vertigo.

Giant ice from eaves at Emigrant Gap grow
upside down. From the mailbox, a returned letter.

At 10, she practiced wading, tried uniform stones
of different sizes, ripped pockets from her jacket.

Evening. I knew there would be dark hawks
crowding that dream instead of rosy doves.

The animal in the road has been there for some time,
appears to be sleeping and looks like a prayer rug.

Weather Change

I'm ready to take my worn notebook to the brackish
water along the creek and stare at the slender sedge.

Sea lions swim this far inland, following salmon.
Folks feed them whitest chunks of Wonder Bread.

In a frenzy, speakers high on matcha tea and sponge
cake soak up all the available open-mike venues.

We move back to the rickety shack. I carve goats
and ravens from Ivory soap. You make rabbit stew.

A closet door is left slightly ajar so Levi's jackets,
old negatives and unopened gifts can freely move.

Ecstasy Before Noon

My day begins with Kathy's blog: a richly toned
Kandinsky, *Composition XI*, a fretwork
of red cellos, purple mandolins, black oboes.

At church, the sermon: "Biblical Academy Awards."
Daniel, cradled in honeyed haunches, saved from the pit's
bone-crunching jaws, earns "Best Live Action."

Sun flames through abstract triangles of crimson
and cobalt glass. An open window to Jerusalem accepts
bluest breezes from drying hills.

A painting by Blake flashes on the overhead screen.
A Rumi poem: *A wave of light builds
in the black pupil of the eye.* No one dozes today.

I cannot suppress a giggle as energetic vibrations
from the organist tremble renaissance shades of heirloom
zinnias in the pewter vase on the simple altar.

Next week in our fellowship hall, Turkish students
from the University will provide a meal to celebrate
the end of Ramadan with dates, lentil soup and prayers.

On the sharing table filled with summer's bounty,
three pearl orbs rest on a white plate, miniature moons glazed
and dusted with lavender stripes, each a Sultan's turban.

Eggplant I'm told. I add yellow tomatoes and lemon cucumber,
what I would have missed had I not woken early
and wondered where I might find beauty.

Ghazal for Bar Soap

Here is a scent to calm, from far away, long ago,
Dy-Dee Doll soap, nipple, diaper, molded hair aglow.

A square, pink and sweet, just guest-sized,
even a jittery child could relax   and flow.

A terry washcloth, small as a stamp, I wash her tiny toes.
She dreams, still wearing her scent   rocking to and fro.

I search modern malls and bath boutiques: maybe wood rose,
frangipani or powdery dust in snow?

I consult aromatherapists for specimens to sample,
even simple oils, but they're too young, too well traveled to know.

At Sephora in Paris, *stimulants de Saug,* a yellowish
body gel—close, but a shade too strange   so

Diane Ackerman hears my plight, forwards Twinkies,
not to eat, just wrappers to sniff   nice and slow.

Maybe garden pools at mountain Zen centers:
baby's breath, fish breath or shiny bubbles to blow?

I write the Society of Brewing Chemists.
They suggest: resinous, warty, pungent steaming sow.

Perhaps the creamy corpse blossoms like the bride's
fuming bouquet in Tim Burton's movie show?

I force-feed the baby, no time to drain. Her chubby
neck and crooked joints leach a black messy goo.

I think of whales waterlogged in kelp much too close to shore.
Hopeful, I'm forever rocking   rocking her   to and fro.

Part III
FRAGMENTS

Aubade for Dark

We come again to loss of night,
sweet velvet shadows, night
with soothing shadows,
time before unfaltering dawn,
unworldly color without
the sweet shadow we call night.

Open all windows that love
can hold. Put your foot against
the first slant obliterating
shadow, violet haze the color of night.

Each year in early spring
two dozen flies spin maniacal
in the clerestory skylight
like winged dominos,
butt heads on the glass, then begin again.

                Hold off
the day's expectation of minutiae,
Larkin's *rented world.*

Why are executions scheduled at dawn
in this incorrigible light?

The comfort of night dwindles into the future;
perishable relics of sleep
hound me through morning hours.

I hurry through the day,
anticipate the glorious sunset seeping
rose-gold shadows.
Yet again, far down the spectrum,
harsh dawn again and flies—fallen.

Inventions

What was the first invention? Double helix,
no big deal, Brother built one with his erector set.

After decades, I replace my vegetable grater,
the new one sharp and still made in America.

My fifth meeting this week, PTA, choir practice.
New minivan. He said: *Don't take your love to town.*

Who would believe the revival of the pressure cooker?
Do they still make the rubber seal and wobbly timer?

Dark, not paying attention, yards of film unravel
onto the floor, the entire history of woman's suffrage.

Returning

Protected in the East, storks are considered pilgrims
    riding the corridor to Mecca.
They remember their birthplace, nest on minarets,
telephone poles, returning again and again
in season's cycles. A pair even lodged
    on the lone pillar of Artemis' temple.

    In a new subdivision,
a poet tells of thumping on her front steps, opens
the door. A wild horse paws the threshold.
Was he born here, did he roam here?

At twelve, my mother sang on the radio:
"When shadows fall and night birds
are ever blending, I am ever wending home."
    Subtle programming?

Ours seems more confused, neighborhoods torn down,
dwellings remodeled by strangers.
I long for my Midwest home, not just the house,
but School #43, Booth's Bookshop, Vonnegut's Hardware.

Like the salmon, I flounder upstream,
struggle on slippery ladders. Yet what happiness.
From the air, I see enclaves, remaining woodlands
    in small clumps near city center.

Salt Lick

Two Black Angus live
in our almond orchard,
get supplements,
but still bury thick heads
in heaps of nuts and hulls.

On moonless evenings
eyes roll upward,
reflect white
beside the glistening salt block.
They do not recognize
night or day. Light
comes from somewhere,
maybe body heat
stamping shapes in darkness.

The butcher comes.
They trot over, swipe
my bare legs with rough tongues,
meat I will later prepare
for the dogs. Our steak
will be tough
and taste like almonds.

American Bittern

A dark eye swivels.
If I had looked away just before,
I would have missed speckled wedges,
chips like a Klimt painting—
bronze, ochre and lime green
    spliced among cattails.
My eye struggles to keep up
with this fleeting image
like imprinting a memory:
    attention-selection-retrieval.
Just a hint, a piece
to build that fear again,
the dark alleyway,
pebbles rattling
deep cracks in the center,
    an overused worry stone.
Or the eye chart, a click of the lens:
blur, fuzz, which memory
is correct, A or B?
Which is better, B or A?
When I leave that thought,
the bittern suddenly thrusts a slow beak
to the sky, becomes a vertical shaft,
one with the reeds, invisible.
The riverbank is quiet.
November grasses in still water
barely move. Colors dissolve
    my blinker's moment.

House of Candlelight

—a cento of sorts

Like a vagrant I wander empty ruins.
Deserted, nothing in sight
but a small opening near dry brush.
With a yellow torch I step inside.
The air, unbelievably dense, darker
than midnight. I turn a corner into an alcove,
part of the stucco sloughed away
except for a dozen saints in russet and blue robes.

A small gap releases dust particles
in sunlight, brings energy and fills earthen jars
with spring water, wakes the images
to a deep listening. They speak
in a foreign tongue, yet clear in meaning.

"We get so tired in winter. We lay down
to stay awake. We do not hear
the flute or tambourine. We cannot smell
the burning aloeswood."
I say to them, "Stars and planets
move to bring grace, clarity
through the cold night." Jesus slips
into a house to escape enemies, opens
the door to another world.
Inside you are sweet beyond telling,
and the cathedral there, so deeply tall.

Night comes so people can sleep
like fish in black water. Underground
streams bleed. Even on dry land
a fish needs to be wrapped in something.
There is a light, a seed grain inside. You are
the mirrors, the faces in it.

Believe me, you are not forgotten.
I know your souls want to walk
into the clearing and not come back.

When I stop speaking this poem
will close and open its silent wings.
The moth is building a house of candlelight.

A Year with Rumi, 2006 (pp. 71, 333, 345, 382, 390)
and *Rumi: The Big Red Book,* 2010 (pp. 18, 65, 66, 168,
280, 371, 402, 470), Coleman Barks.

Waste Ground

So tempting to reach down and extract
greasy food wrappers, a torn pink
laundry basket, strips of rubber tires.
But, remembering our brain's reuptake system,
sucking up, storing, recycling spent chemicals
from narrow synapses for further use,

I just observe this misshapen outline,
this derelict ground: soil heaps from mine workings,
a land with no name where birds used to sing,
broken typewriters, busted lunch pails,
rotting lumber and rusty nails,
cracked foundations like citadels,
tunnels, remnants of demolished buildings,
and just enough sunlight to stir
old sugars into action,
phosphates made moldy in canning jars.

    Worms begin to reappear.

And, there—gardens blooming,
staking their own claim: Scarlet Pimpernel,
Curled Dock, Groundsel and Speedwell.
Smell the fruited Pineapple Weed,
feel soft Mouse Ear against your leg,
hear Bindweed pods rattle at the setting sun,
dip your hand into Shepherd's Purse,
    touch a few cool farthings.

This is not a dream—simply soil remaking itself,
the gift of reclamation, a modern-day midden.

Fragments

> What was scattered gathers
> What was gathered blows apart
> —Heraclitus, 500 B.C.

As air stirs ocean
breath infuses breath;
the coastline retreats,
food again plentiful.
> *What was scattered gathers.*

The sky solidifies
as rooftop to the world;
glass transforms
into a million faceted beads.
> *What was gathered blows apart.*

The mountain you rest on
rebuilds itself from shifting lava.
You must find a new dune,
lie prostrate above Drake's Bay.
> *What was scattered gathers.*

The channel we thought too deep
is now a shallow meander.
The Russian River splits its tongue
and enters the Pacific.
> *What was gathered blows apart.*

Cosmos trumps chaos;
the preacher tries again
on the hillsides of Ephesus.
Attentive pilgrims face east.
> *What was scattered gathers.*

Mythology

—a contemporary haibun

Today we visit Troy. Some call it sparse,
boring, gone to ruin. But I look
forward to placing my feet where Helen
strode, then fled (so the story goes).

I walk in rubble, follow the visitor's path
along rickety wood hand rails. Rain begins on a slant.
I duck under the archeologist's tarp shaped
like one huge Phoenician sail.
   The wind billows, inflates.

I'm drawn back to *The Iliad*
and Hector's words: *Honor the gods.*
Love your woman. Defend your country.

The information plaque states:
"Ten or more layers of antiquity discovered."
The rain stops. I walk on, wonder
about my own sketchy mythology.
Perhaps I will find a hidden well,
   waters still sweetened by remnants
of Anatolian tulips.

I let my imaginary bucket down
like a game of chance
at the neighborhood carnival,
hope for a precious relic and there...

   ivory bulbs thrust from archaic humus,
   rise eight inches, flesh-toned and wet.

   Sky clears blue. I want to stay but must
   hurry on to reach the Dardanelles by dusk.

Helen at the Scaean Gate

—Painting, Gustave Moreau

Sun-splashed walls blister
crimson: blast of gold on stone.
Stone for the ages bathes in enduring luster,
everything at right angles except the blue fabric sky.
The only movement, the curvature
of gray smoke from smoldering fires;
the only sound, fragments
in the censer breaking apart.
A few peasants gather near the entrance,
obscured in brown shadows.
Helen in midnight blue and ivory,
chalk face featureless: just as well.
Outside the weakest gate, she stands on a hillock,
looks away from the entrance to Troy,
perhaps keeps watch over women
who go to the quiet spring to launder tattered garments.
Helen's arm holds the lamp that faces the sea.
Pillar of inspiration or fallible weakness,
she stands like an Ionian column
as if already enshrined at a World Heritage Site.
She has no words for us. She had
her chance, refused to identify a king's enemies.
She will no longer taste meaty oranges from Spain.
In the long afternoon of Troy's brilliance,
she will go back inside, nothing to do but wait
for ships that will not come.
There is so much missing here.
In the censer her afterthoughts drift as lace,
then burn clean, epics turned to ash.

Metropolitan

It was important then to be tasteful—
mirrored tiles, gold-streaked
or gray-smoked, a popular item.

Used extensively on dining room
walls, such a touch of elegance,
1970s version of *savoir faire.*

Friends hosted a dinner party—
game hens, the stuffing rich
with caraway seeds and brown rice.
I glanced at our images.

Mirrors obscured faces, difficult-
to-see intimate interactions.
We talked through fog.

Some would think the little squared
reflections a source of comfort;
instead the surface
appeared impenetrable.

I watched the clock and noticed
puffy black stars emerging
from a gold-flecked ceiling.

Frond Ghazal

Are you the great relentless one, searching
words, volumes, reduced to a limping iamb?

There is no race to exit, only the one in my cortex.
I stop to inscribe the chalked memory of a thrush.

Seas relax, putrid air purifies with violet, brambles
hiding the walk clear themselves. The vaccines work.

Over the next hill, a noisy bonfire? or just Lot's
wife burning saline, new dew caught in tired goatskins.

It will take years to walk all the fronds inside this palm
until we reach the steppes, the savannas, the Solomons.

Part IV
FOOT STONES

Breast Reliefs

We do not know if lips were full
or features broad and planetary.

Found among broken frescos
in the shallow waters of Lake Constance,

red ochre breasts survived,
ivory circles still vivid.

Evidence tells she lived in a land
of copper, emmer and poppies.

Was she clothed in flax
or nude, draped in a golden girdle?

Did hands hold a delicate lamp,
the sacred conch or tankard of dark amber?

We do know this sculptor loved women.
Experience formed these dense breasts

like Persian melons
at summer solstice.

     I think of Sappho—
   such longing in a fragment.

Abundance of Light

Such a thick candle
and other yellowed things,
the lesson of morning certain.

Melted tallow.
Which sputters,
flame or dark wick?

Running is to flee
the last vivid dreams
set to rage—now pause.

Skies given, the arm
raises prematurely,
disturbs nebula's white fire,

pushes outward
the corona of gift,
dawn breath, moist with
waiting and want.

Emily said,
When it comes,
the landscape listens.

Each day begins: milky
profusion, abundant shadow,
the slim glimmer of morning.

Kelp

It can happen on a vacant shore
You watch a man walk toward you focused
on the sea beyond. Tan, a hot pecan.
Gorgeous in lavender shirt,
black trunks, his face broad as a god's.

Not young, not old, hair a mix
of gray whorls as he avoids
the spiny sponge and slips in.

I enter, say "How beautiful your skin,"
happy to share the same deep blue.
He opens to butterfly,
surf crinkling deep-set eyes.

This must be what Poseidon looks like:
rivulets, pores and foam, and with each
forward movement, air mixes with
the scent of sweet cloves and pungent cumin.

He moves further out. Not a strong swimmer,
I sidestroke following his gaze.
Behind, he leaves a rich carnelian burn,
a red rash cutting the sea.
Salt spray sears my eyes. I look away, stumble,
tangle in kelp, slip and falter.

Almost drowning, how did I come to this?
Was it the "Song of India,"
"In the Steppes of Central Asia" (Borodin?),
or the Omar Bread man's warm cinnamon rolls?

Calico

I buy a thrift store blouse,
the old "Sacred Threads" brand,
patchwork rayon, multiflowered prints
mostly faded to pinks
and greens similar to my shirt
sold at the garage sale years ago,
life in shambles along with crockpots
and faded tents, tables crammed with mementos,
the worn family games the saddest:
Monopoly, Scrabble, Chutes and Ladders.
"Fillers," someone said; pastimes.
I saved the bag of runic stones.
The little ovals still grate against each other
in their velvet bag. I toss,
decipher: partnership (self), flow (tides)
and change (passage).
The thrift store blouse holds
a few bright calicos,
the wood buttons strong, stitches secure.
One thing I can do:
mend the tiny hole near the pocket.

The Sound of Snow

A wet snow, lush like a kiss, soon melts.
Dry snow, crisp as a sharp word,
stays on the ground, piles up
in berms, in dreams, in afterimages.

At the bay window, the first drift,
cold enough to stick.
I'm certain I hear a frenzy, flakes cascading
or straight on like Midwest blizzards.

They told us no two snowflakes
are alike: each exists as an intricate
individual. In reality, über-techno photos
report a few basic patterns.

       I think
the sound I hear is each one searching
for its template, each starburst seeking,
finding, easing into its parchment-scented mate.

Adornments

On each russet-colored step, I'm greeted
by a scattering of rose petals. A page
falls open to tracings of Buddha's foot stones.
I'm overwhelmed by a single icon,
could write an entire sequence
from an eagle feather or filaments of spider webs.
The stones are filled with sun mandalas,
fire wheels, chariots to the nether world.
One circlet has sprouted wings,
a forced-air emblem. Two fish
nose up, quiver translucent celadon scales.
I take my magnifier and discover
a cocoon or perhaps a miniature mummy
lucky charm. On one heel, a mountain
near explosion set to ignite from a false step.
Flames sear on toes, grasp
for oxygen. If I were to adorn my own feet,
I might choose the wings like leaves, symbolic of my love
for trees. I might choose a mountain
for the memory of my hike up the Denali.
I would choose a simpler mandala, not the Eastern
style used for meditation, so full of bursting lotuses
and prancing elephants. Mine would be
basic, my shadow in the center
as I wait for the white snake to creep down.
A few additions: a butterfly and snow in a pewter bowl.
The crescent moon is also welcome—Moon,
my mother's name to remind me of the eternal
feminine, the strong and arched fallopian.
Glancing again at his feet, I would not include
the chalice. It's been overdone, and already found.

I would not include the swastikas
on the other toes. They have seen too much.
The rose petals on the porch have blown away.
I may still capture them, soft-scented
and curled under my feet, my own foot stones.

> *Buddha Foot Stones.* Tracings from the T'ient-t'ai
> Monastery in Peiping, China.

At the Ruins

A man is a god in ruins. —Emerson

Humid today, still the air
smells of sun and dust.
We walk past
the remains of Zeus' temple.

A sarcophagus yawns open
with yet another Medusa carving.
Always fascinating
what remnants remain
from wars, earthquakes, aging.

Along the road,
locals sell goods and wares.
A young family displays
honey and figs. I give them a coin
for their photo.
Our guide says,
"See that old woman to the left?
Twenty years ago she cheated someone.
Don't buy from her."

In tatters, she sells baby booties knitted
in bright polyester colors and faded
scarves hanging from an olive tree.

I don't buy anything,
but give her a coin because
she endures, because
she lives among the gods.

Western Turkey, 2012

Manikin

In a childhood diary I found a replica,
a few inches tall, blue ink on stiff cardboard,
curly hair and legs fashioned to a point.
She grasped a bouquet like the one in a Chagall painting.
Spritely, I could have plucked her out
of *A Midsummer Night's Dream.*
Was she my alter ego,
a little muse, or simply a bookmark?

At the pizza parlor, five-year-old Jim put a quarter
in the slot for a two-inch plastic "stretch man."
Eyes and nose the only features,
yet when you pulled
his face grew into a smile.
Jim laid him next to his warm pepperoni
and frothy root beer, a safe friend who
would not spit on him or call him names,
who could travel in daydreams to summer ponds,
skip stones and catch polliwogs.

Carl Jung carved his "little man" from the tip of a ruler,
face inked black, complete with frock coat,
hat and shiny boots.
Hidden inside a yellow pencil case,
an entire universe took shape: a wool sock
for a bed, a stone from the Rhine
divided in half with bright paint
like an aboriginal shield,
and a tiny library with scrolls
and secret codes that explained feelings,
that gave him courage when criticized
for time spent on books.
Manikin carried all his burdens.
Jung later wondered, was the little fellow
just a strip of wood or actually a miniature god?

Cave of Forgotten Dreams

—film, Werner Herzog

Present-day vineyards, a pristine cult sealed
by a rockslide, flash frozen in time, spatial
points filmed by photographers on low gurneys.

Like a curio cabinet, fragments gather: cave bear skull,
cracked hand, the smallest phalange missing,

and a surprise butterfly
holding remnants of red.

Green oxygen profiles; a horse whimpers.
This is Chauvet Cave, the Dordogne.

How to make sense of a woman's lower half,
so many open mouths, animals in a fury,
the entire gallery near erasure from toxic ozone.

This *grotte*, this throat so silent for 28,000 years.
Yet, here, a pentatonic flute carved from
a vulture's wing, the type still used in Germany.

At the nearby nuclear plant on the Rhône River,
albino crocodiles blinded by residual
chemicals flourish in vast cooling ponds.

I ask, "What icons have we evolved here, so close
to subterranean dreams, trapped in splintered fissures?"

The ground above is scented in wild thyme
and covered with ivy. It is fitting the soundtrack
is filled with Wagner's melodies, a deep reach
embellishing these inner landscapes.

Kabir hears a flute but does not know whose tune it is.

Vibrations

In the middle of the night I ask again,
"Do you hear it?" Not the engines from McClellan Field,
nor the fridge, its gentle hum. Something
      of earth or sky, or both?
Over the Aegean, a quarter moon and single star
spangle in dawn's early light.
A smart man once said, "Heaven is today, not yesterday
and not tomorrow" (sorry you missed it).
I look up the Aramaic word for heaven: *Shemeya*
(sacred vibrations, never ending).
And when I think complete silence, again, the pulse
of a *million suns,* the *slip of comet's tail*—
      immeasurable.
I want to find heaven on earth, a glimpse of kindness
in the everyday. An Arab country gave
our students new computers when tornadoes damaged
their Midwest school. Think back to the joy
almost missed at lunch, corona of noonday sun
over your office building, the photo
you snapped with your cellphone. The constant
reaching takes solitude and a pause, the empty table,
a glass of water. I wept when a few bees
returned to deep cones of white prairie flowers,
hovering in golden pollen, shaking loose
golden abundance in midair. I was told to watch
for attractors, great and small. Do we know
the pull of a hummingbird's wing, the moon's constant tug?
All vibrations serve: the squirrel's
tiny muscle quivers as he buries a last something
in the flower bed. The friendly worm's long stretch,
wisp of slow arch,
      reenters the earth.
Pinecones smack our metal roof, your measured
sleep and cool breath on my pillow.

In the Sierras with Rumi

October sky, alpine lakes strike crystal.
Aspens quiver heart shapes above buttery moss.
Not much talking among the Stellar's jays.
Hooked-jaw kokanee spawn scarlet,
become friends with glory.

Black bears give out the big yawn;
we anticipate snow.
Behind the local college,
a mountain lion is seen crossing the swale,
barely visible among golden weeds.

Rumi, you want to escape your ego,
lose yourself in the mountains.
I recommend shoes. I will bring my shawl.

If you believe snowforms do not last through July,
I can show you the deep crevice above the tree line.
You want to find inland whales?
I can show you the darker side of Granite Peak.

We wonder about time and fill our eyes
with ancient redwoods, the old gods.

In the Truckee Meadows, river birch count stiff rings.
We see what we see, discuss beginnings.
You know, embryo,
you must recognize the difference
between solitude and desolation.

If we lose ourselves in the mountains,
if we take a wrong turn, we can sit like the Washoe,
toss knuckles onto a blanket, find our way.

You said there was a mountain range inside your chest.
Look east from the summit, there, Nevada—
a smooth plain with antelope.

A Moment of Joy

Photo: Altaf Qadri, New Delhi, Associated Press

Collage
    of rubble—
abandoned plastic bottles

    odd table with oilcloth
lopsided tent   old rubber tires

    various shades of stain
no foliage in sight.

But here, a girl
      7 or 8 finds
a piece of rope—
    skips barefoot

happy, slap-slap
cutting her above the rest
        airborne

hair rising like flames
—a smile cracking
      the universe.

Five Nudes

My lens lights on curvature,
David's torso a lit candelabra, overlarge veins
pulsed and ready. Fabled eyes wonder
if the sling will hold. At cardinal points,
close-ups fill the frame: four nudes glisten
ebony gloss, delicate scarab.
I imagine private inscriptions hidden beneath.

Do they bow in praise to retrieve the stone
that reached heaven,
or kneel to save more errant pebbles?
More like a cathedral than a museum,
there could be hymns of praise,

    "Who from our Mother's arms,
    hath blessed us on our way,"

but in the far mosaic, the lyre stands quiet.

Twilight, a hot July, a rooftop dinner.
I will remember the duration of 400 years,
ancient marble, multiple shanks,
not rough-cut but new willows, shorn and green.

I don't know the curator's intent.
I'm only here with my own need,
still a beggar before beauty.

> *Perfection in Form, Michelangelo's David and
> Mapplethorpe's Photos.* Exhibit, Galleria dell Academia,
> Florence 2009

Stars of the Summer Triangle

I'm writing on the patio
of a small café;
crushed scent of cumin from the kitchen

makes my mind wander to thoughts
of you: you, finely tuned, muscular,
deep brown eyes under graying brows.

(How long has it been? A month? A year?)

The old iron chair I sit on,
rough, colors raspy with rust;

sharp edges dig into my leg,
slightly painful but necessary to aging.

And I'm thinking this was good,
a transitory infatuation.

Samosas arrive, steaming with another
sauce: darker, tangy, Tangier.

Minotaur Surprised while Eating

—Painting, Maddi Hambling

All light reflects the pale, hairless torso,
paper-thin skin, frail blue shadows bleeding,

delicate chest and arms, like one
not used to day labor or butchery.

This man part seems too small above
chunky fur legs, the split, steel hooves.

A bit of flesh dangles from wet lips,
a crimson haunch glistening raw,

just the right amount of marbling.
A thick flank:

    ibex, gazelle?

His eyes beg forgiveness,
the embarrassment clear.

In the fading orange and blue sky,
a tilt of his head seems to incriminate.

I give pardon as I check my own prehensile hands,
remember the crush of pine,

the many times I tore flesh from the great
pike in the fish shack in northern Minnesota.

Retrieval

Another episode, my life another window,
each episode a dream. Wild flowers, if they are wild,
feverfew, wolfsbane, remain open under the constant moon
and summer rains. If it is summer, weeds are predictable,
splashing parchment on old fields.

I want the dream, the same recurring dream, and full streams,
childhood streams: "Little Ripple" and "Cobbler's Creek."
And I am there in worn sandals on grassy banks wondering
again why people return to the same dream.

My brother stationed in Iran for six years
learned Farsi and planted roses.
Camels ate the roses. On weekends,
soldiers filled jeeps with gas, drove through the desert
past ancient civilizations. The tank half-empty,
they returned to base. He still dreams
he can't leave that country.

If only I could walk again into that reverie
with no disruptions, no spongy meadow, no washed-out bridges
hanging in midair. All citrine yellow, the abandoned
lot next to my childhood movie theater fills
with broken hypodermics.
Each episode unfolds into the next.
That part of memory that needs procedures—
I know that route, where to turn,
which alleyway to hurry past at midnight.
Emerson said "Every word was once
a poem." Early semantics or seminal dreams?

Memory circles back, retrieves wild flowers
and summer squalls, readjusts rivulets that take out
footpaths, picks up today's data and reconstructs my life
to include the scarlet pimpernel. In the avalanche
of memories, my streams search for new valleys.

The Sultan's Ballroom

Above ancient outcrops,
a distant loud speaker,
the muezzin's call to prayer.

At a roadside stand, I admire Aladdin's lamps,
tarnished but standing out among brass trinkets.
Yes, this will be magical.

From the bus window a sign,
"The Sultan's Ballroom," over an ornate building.
I recall my harem costume, wide fuchsia-
colored pants like the ones in odalisque paintings.

When I get to the dance floor, perhaps a folk ensemble
will play *Ali Pasa, Gudi,* or *Oy Memo,*
Turkish dances I'm familiar with,
movements I already know.

Or maybe on a side street,
a lesser club, a caliph's taverna,
more intimate, not so touristy—
perhaps a rhumba in blousy pantaloons.

I asked Ahmet,
"What time does the ballroom open?"

"Early, reservations are required.
And it is balloons!
Check website if you want
to schedule a ride on hot air."

                Cappadocia, Turkey

Angels in Summer

I believe angels exist in hot weather
to keep an eye on Queen Anne's lace,
inhale vapors of Spanish moss,
harness shooting stars,
pick truffles emerging from dark loam:
all the things they own.

Angels relish the taste of salt that forms
on work shirts, snitch remnants
of doilies from the bargain table,
gather all the white petals that drop
in June moonlight, rush
to sprinkle new dew on furry toadstools.

They want to weave gossamer from webs
of August into new wings for winter,
scour recycle bins for bits of organdy to snip
into flakes for the first flurries.

You see, these are not God's major angels,
who are too busy with myth;
these are lesser angels taking temp work:
available only in summer.

If I could give a flavor to angels in mid-July,
it would be pineapple sherbet.

Moth and Lace

In this restored "gold country" hotel,
I relax near a frosted window
    etched with rosebuds.

Along the ivory casement, a moth hooks
in curtains, body trapped in a bed of parchment lace.

I look away, try to ignore the myth—
love-distraction-flame—move
to the veranda with my coffee and scones.

Near the chipped bannister,
I sit quiet in another kind of light.
The fragrance of summer; how tangled
the yellow honeysuckle,
    how easy to be fooled.

Just yesterday, in my garden,
a dragonfly perched on the ambergris
metal frog, like a brass ornament
    soldered to the tip.
When I looked again,
he slipped away, taking his fragile body
    to another world. I wonder
at things that move so quickly
we don't even notice.

Rumi says, "You can judge a moth
by the beauty of its candle."
I wonder at a great love unnurtured,
untended like ivy,
    so invasive it lifts tiles
from the roof or snakes leafy tendrils
into the hearth to dry and incite fires.

Have I missed something?
I go inside and shake the curtain.
The moth is gone, taking the most important
    words written on tiny feet.

Grass Valley, California

Genome Project

Frost in April, roses blooming, global warning?
Time is short, we age, we ache to know.

Rush to identify features carried
by golden finches, then dispersed like chaff!

Fractured mosaics struggle to mimic
facts explained in the master plan:

striped cells for smell, digestion and bone:
little structures modified by recent evolution.

I hear Persia provides cardamom.
Let's paint the body for surgery!

Skin is tough enough, holds long bones;
    duct tape keeps parts secure.

Why am I built like a Nuer woman?
How many cows will my family give for this bride?

Glaciers shrink. We drink heartily from udders.
Listen to meat sizzling on open spits,

remnants of animal fat and torchless eyes before flint!
An old candle in my pantry—*Identify the scent!*

Drawers with odd buttons, beeswax, snipped
labels and dust   rest   content without origins.

Ordovician

Glass Beach below Fort Bragg
holds remnants from the refuse site:
green, rose and clear.
Perhaps gems from Asia made beautiful
by salt churning, tumbling gloss.

On Irish sand, I found a Japanese tea cup
broken yet shiny. Can tart crystals
be a curative, grit toughen,
polish me, grind
rough edges smooth
and less worrisome?
And what to think of brittle sea stars
methodically regenerating breakable arms?
Heaven's master plan or burned-out relic?

Here, the Russian River meets the Pacific.
I'm humbled as I watch the 400-million-year retreat
of inland seas, Ordovician remnants.
I'm relieved: I don't have to see
Kansas as a mere island with jawless fish.

Water wrinkles indentations,
puckers appear, small forms breathe.
A limpet travels on one fleshy foot.
Shoreline as ecstasy—
salt thrums reveries, resets blood flow,
reboots my nervous system
to pen, paper,
beyond pictorial dictionaries.

Slow Snapshots from a Fast-Moving Train

We lost the sleeper car east of Denver.
I did enjoy the morning paper
and rosebud on the breakfast tray,
the porter returning with a silver coffee pot.

I settle for an overlarge lounge chair,
spend time at the window
or in the dome car at sunrise
reading John Haines' *Winter News.*

The Zephyr heads west, climbs the plateau
where the Cheyenne made winter camp,
circular depressions still visible, a long habitation.

Ahead, I imagine German POWs
working the ice fields. I curl
under my thermal blanket from home.

Two days out the toilets begin to plug.
The deli runs out of sandwiches.

We pass red-roofed Glenwood Springs,
where Doc Holliday coughed
into a last handkerchief.

The club car closes at midnight.
We make a brief stop on the edge
of Salt Lake City. The young man who spends
most of his time with a beer jumps down,

runs ½ mile to the 7-Eleven for a six-pack he cannot
bring on board. He spends his
remaining hours pacing dark aisles.

In daylight we travel past a turquoise lake.
The Donner Party still sleeps in deep snow,
their wagons lashed for a final trip over the summit.

Closer to the Sacramento Depot, I note under a culvert
an ironing board covered in flowered fabric,
no power among scattered belongings.

Home, I wake at 3 a.m. to the train's wail,
think of all the lost looking for a place to rest.
I have no knowledge of life
without a pillow or weary head on stone.
Yet we must all drift
to the same dream: white canyons,
amulet guarding an open door, worn threshold,
spoon by the plate, the same dream.

After a Few Years

You're in the village, somewhere.
If I wandered small streets, I might see you,
still robust but older,
coming out of the library
or in the coffeehouse reading Colette.

Only a glimpse.
We would meld into others,
two at the same point in time, checking clocks,
wanting more time, or having
too much time.

Once we went to the shore
for lunch like so many others.
Now, at Redondo Pier,
I wonder.
Eating fried prawns like the ones we loved,
walking the beach, phosphorescent waves
looping in, I see your eyes,
liquid blue—
your face suntanned,
rimmed in solar flares,
swimming swiftly toward me.

Prufrock at the Coast

> What little we have ever understood is like an offering
> we make beside the sea. —Ursula Le Guin

When you've been too long inland, you wonder
which beach it will be, the crowded one
with no entrance fee,
or the one at the bottom of a craggy bluff.
You decide on the flat one, toilets
and a $7 senior discount.
The sign says, "Rip Currents Unsafe!"
You didn't plan on swimming anyway,
just came to walk, sit and watch.
You've heard the sand is good for feet, cool, soft
and spongy, a wet caramel color.
At the far end, waves crack dark boulders,
you sit in late summer salt spray, sticky and sweet.
Suddenly, aggressive tide laps and sucks
at your beach chair. Returning on cracked shells,
stones and smooth glass, it's slow going
but you pick your way, stimulating, painful
like a giant pinch or a lit match held
to ascertain consciousness or sleepwalking.
The fog is in, visibility low.
You put on your sandals, pink feet full of cuts,
and attempt to make a still life from orange seaweed,
a gull's feather, crab claw and twisted
driftwood, *nature morte*, but the dun colors
are too boring, too reflective of your drab life.
Yet you were lucky to avoid
sleeper waves and strong backwash.
This feather, in its whiteness and strength,
you save between the pages of a book.

Notes

p. 2 "A Soft Garden," some phrases by Rumi.

p. 5 "In Tarsus," from a photo by Greg Chalpin.

p. 14 "An Invitation," first line by Rumi.

p. 16 "Preference," after Jim Harrison, XL.

p. 22 "Prayer Rug Ghazal," after Jim Harrison, XLII.

p. 26 "Aubade," quote, Philip Larkin.

p. 33 "Waste Ground," inspired by *Nicholson's Plants of the British Isles.*

p. 39 "Breast Reliefs," from a photo, Archeology, 1993.

p. 42 "Vibrations," quotes, Walt Whitman, Gerard Manley Hopkins.

p. 47 "Manikin," after Carl Jung, *Memories, Dreams, and Reflections.*

p. 59 "After a Few Years," in the style of Dick Allen.

Acknowledgments

Artifact: "Barefoot," "Ghazal for Bar Soap," "Genome Project"
Blue Fifth Review: "Vibrations"
Brevities: "Hodja's Story"
Centrifugal Eye: "Mythology"
Connecticut River Review: "A Moment of Joy"
Convergence: "Moth and Lace," "Prufrock at the Coast"
Cooweescoowee: "Angels in Summer"
Cosumnes River Journal: "Salt Lick"
Edge: "Edging Exotic into Consciousness"
Ekphrasis: "Breast Reliefs"
Forge Journal: "Mary's House," "At the Ruins," "Petition,"
    "Brunch Ghazal," "A Soft Garden," "In Istanbul," "In the Sierras
    with Rumi," "Prayer Rug Ghazal," "Frond Ghazal," "In Tarsus,"
    "Stars of the Summer Triangle"
The MacGuffin: "New Delhi"
Medusa's Kitchen: "Ecstasy Before Noon"
North Dakota Quarterly: "Swimming in the Aegean"
Poppy Road Journal: "Wintering Mushrooms," "Metropolitan"
Rosebud: "Slow Snapshots from a Fast-Moving Train"
Sentinel Poetry Review: "Where the River Fans Out,"
    "Arabesque"
West Trestle Review: "What a Poem Can Do"
The Whirlwind Review: "Returning"

"Pergamum Altar" and "Waste Ground" were included in the
chapbook, *The Meaning of Monoliths,* Poet's Corner Press, 2006.

"New Delhi" won the MacGuffin Poet Hunt, 2013.

"Salt Lick" won the Bay Area Poet's Coalition Award, 2009.

"Where the River Fans Out" won third prize from *Sentinel Poetry
Quarterly* (UK), 2013.

"Slow Snapshots from a Fast Moving Train" was one of two finalists
for the William Stafford Poetry Award, 2014.

The author is also grateful to the Squaw Valley Community
of Writers for providing an atmosphere of experimentation and
risk-taking, the Cenacle Retreat House for all things mystical,
Ananda Village for inspiration and solitude, the Cache Creek Nature
Preserve for the beauty of California streams and riparian enclaves.
She especially wants to thank Tom Goff and Russell Thorburn for
the thoughtful consultations and arrangement of the manuscript
and her poetry friends: St. Mark's Scribes, Third Sunday Writers
and Morning Coffee Salon. Also the Sacramento Poetry Center and
the Lake Tahoe poetry community for their continuing support.

Cover *artwork, "Pergamum Altar" by Norma Maienknecht;
author photo by Greg Chalpin; cover and interior book design
by Diane Kistner; Liberation Serif text with Avant Garde titling*

About FutureCycle Press

FutureCycle Press is dedicated to publishing lasting English-language poetry books, chapbooks, and anthologies in both print-on-demand and Kindle ebook formats. Founded in 2007 by long-time independent editor/publishers and partners Diane Kistner and Robert S. King, the press incorporated as a nonprofit in 2012. A number of our editors are distinguished poets and writers in their own right, and we have been actively involved in the small press movement going back to the early seventies.

The FutureCycle Poetry Book Prize and honorarium is awarded annually for the best full-length volume of poetry we publish in a calendar year. Introduced in 2013, our Good Works projects are anthologies devoted to issues of universal significance, with all proceeds donated to a related worthy cause. Our Selected Poems series highlights contemporary poets with a substantial body of work to their credit; with this series we strive to resurrect work that has had limited distribution and is now out of print.

We are dedicated to giving all of the authors we publish the care their work deserves, making our catalog of titles the most diverse and distinguished it can be, and paying forward any earnings to fund more great books.

We've learned a few things about independent publishing over the years. We've also evolved a unique, resilient publishing model that allows us to focus mainly on vetting and preserving for posterity poetry collections of exceptional quality without becoming over-whelmed with bookkeeping and mailing, fundraising activities, or taxing editorial and production "bubbles." To find out more about what we are doing, come see us at www.futurecycle.org.

The FutureCycle Poetry Book Prize

All full-length volumes of poetry published by FutureCycle Press in a given calendar year are considered for the annual FutureCycle Poetry Book Prize. This allows us to consider each submission on its own merits, outside of the context of a contest. Too, the judges see the finished book, which will have benefitted from the beautiful book design and strong editorial gloss we are famous for.

The book ranked the best in judging is announced as the prize-winner in the subsequent year. There is no fixed monetary award; instead, the winning poet receives an honorarium of 20% of the total net royalties from all poetry books and chapbooks the press sold online in the year the winning book was published. The winner is also accorded the honor of being on the panel of judges for the next year's competition; all judges receive copies of all contending books to keep for their personal library.

www.ingramcontent.com/pod-product-compliance
Lightning Source LLC
Chambersburg PA
CBHW070004100426
42741CB00012B/3115